Ricky Roogle

THE USELESS BOOK
The absurd activity book

The use les s book

The absurd activity book

A short history of this book

Operating instructions:
Complete all tasks as described in the book.
Create new experiments by extending or modifying the tasks.
Never leave this book unattended! Take it along everywhere.
Work through it from front to back, from back to front or simply criss-cross!

Pull it through!

Safety Notice & Preface:
Please note that playing through the tasks in this book can lead to messy or unclean results (dirt, rubbish etc.). Don't be surprised if you get wet or if your table or clothes show more paint stains or glue marks than before.
The further you get, the more disastrous the condition of the book will be. However, the better you master the tasks, the more you will notice a new creative power within yourself which may make the tiring tastes of everyday life a little more exciting.

Bibliographic information of the German National Library:
The German National Library lists this publication in the German National Bibliography; detailed bibliographic data are available on the Internet at http://dnb.dnb.de.

© 2022 Ricky Roogle;1st edition
Cover art, text & illustrations © 2022 Ricky Roogle
Author contact: ricky.roogle@t-online.de
Production and publisher: BoD - Books on Demand

ISBN: 9783756227372

TAKE A HOLE PUNCH AND PUNCH AWAY ALL THE DOTS ON THIS PAGE! FOLD OR CREASE THE SHEET TO REACH THE INDIVIDUAL DOTS.

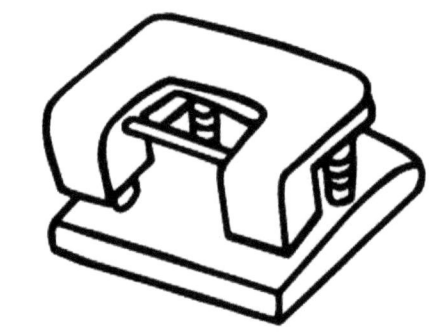

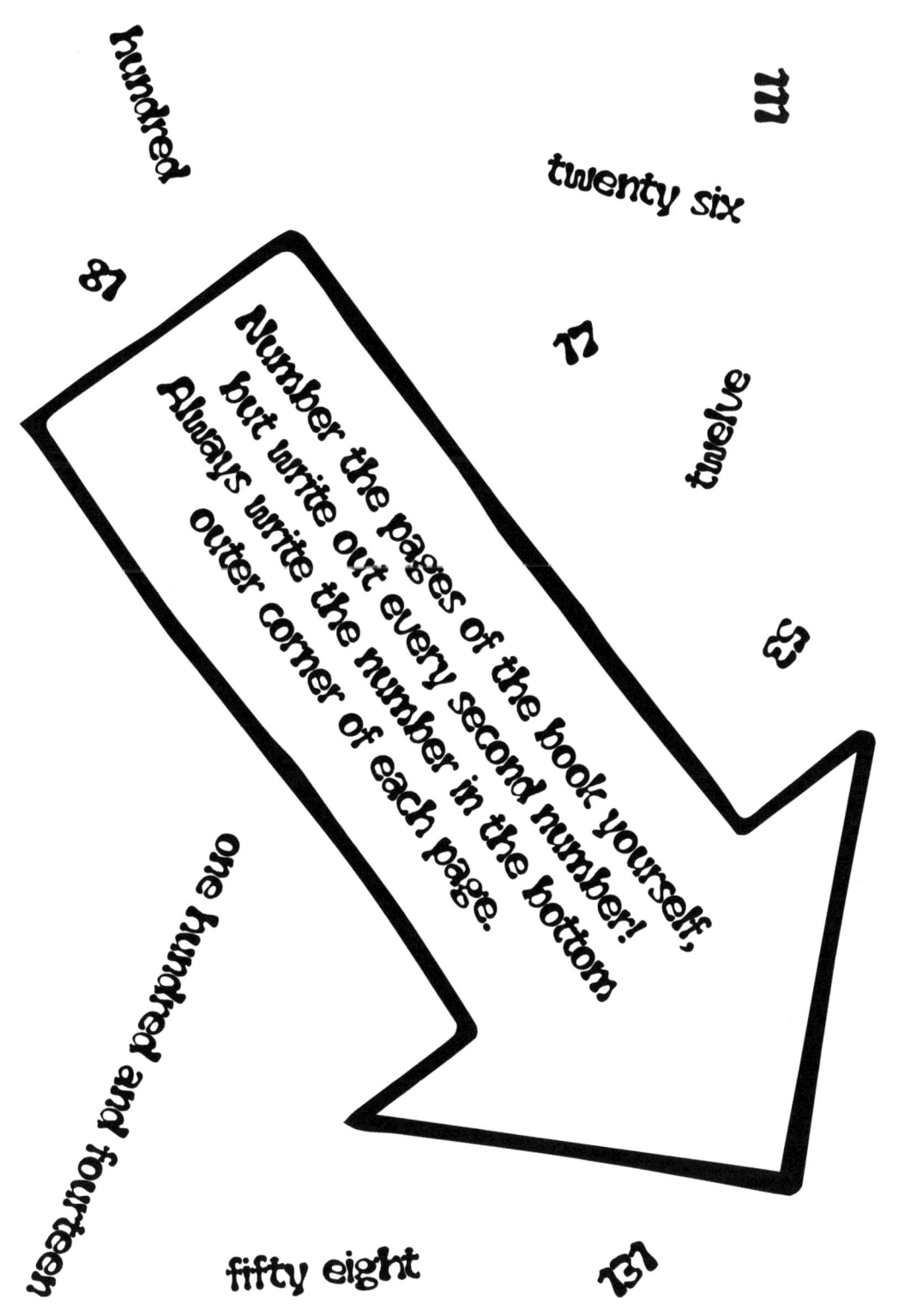

Number the pages of the book yourself,
but write out every second number!
Always write the number in the bottom
outer corner of each page.

hundred

m

twenty six

13

17

twelve

83

one hundred and fourteen

fifty eight

157

137

Dip your thumb in red ink and make numerous thumbprints on this page!

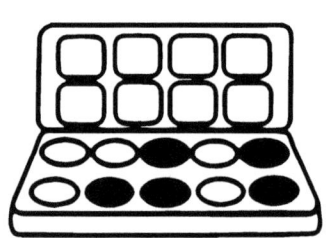

SCRIBBLE QUESTION MARKS WHILE SOMEONE IS TALKING TO YOU!

Hold the book high above your head with one hand and draw three straight lines on this page with the other hand!

1st line   2nd line   3rd line

ALTERNATIVELY, YOU CAN ALSO GLUE IT.. SEW A BUTTON ON THIS SIDE

Glue stick

Say nothing for the next three minutes! Paint one dot per second and keep to this rythm!

Ask someone you know well to draw a scary monster in the picture frame.

Take a stapler and staple connecting lines between the dots!
Fold or crease the sheet to reach the dots.

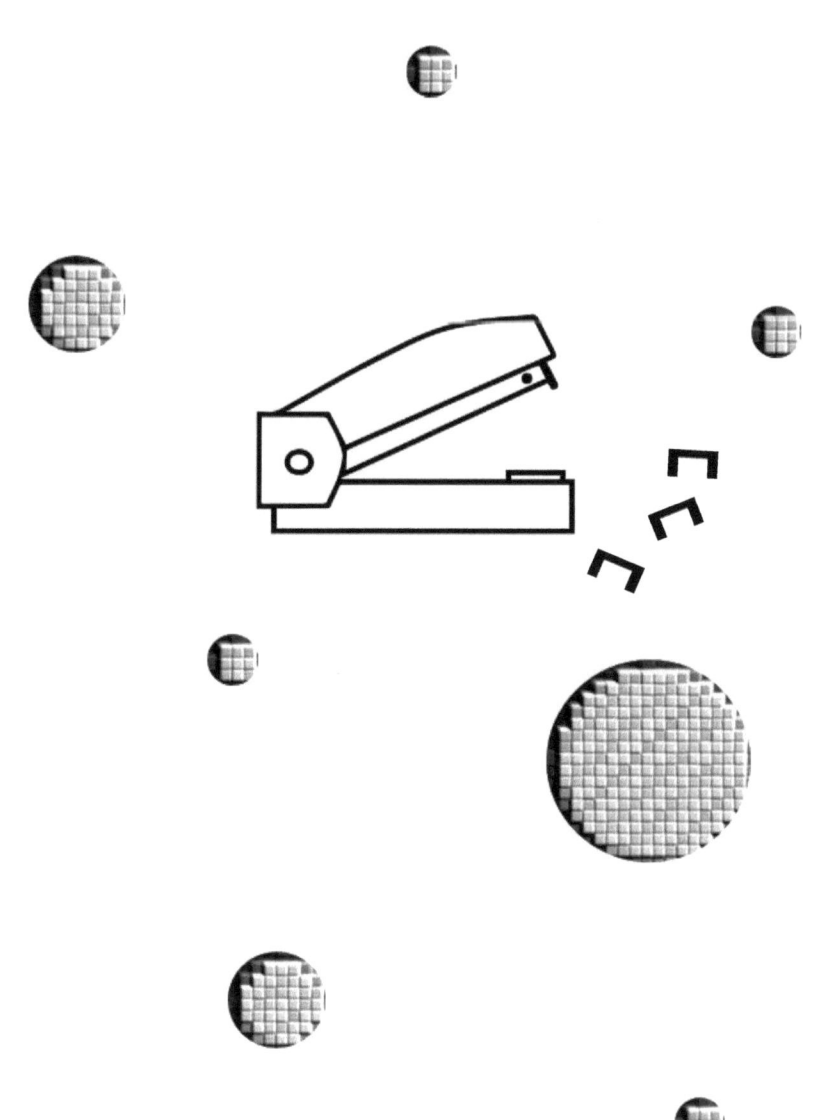

Remove the page from the
book.
Cut it up into the smallest
pieces you manage.
Then draw a laughing moon
face with a glue on the next
but one page.
Afterwards scatter the snippets
over the picture with the still
fresh glue so that many of the
snippets stick to the page.

Glue stick

Paint the laughing moon face here with the glue stick and then sprinkle the snippets over it.

The glue with the snippets should be completely dried up before you continue.

PAINT YOUR INDEX FINGER

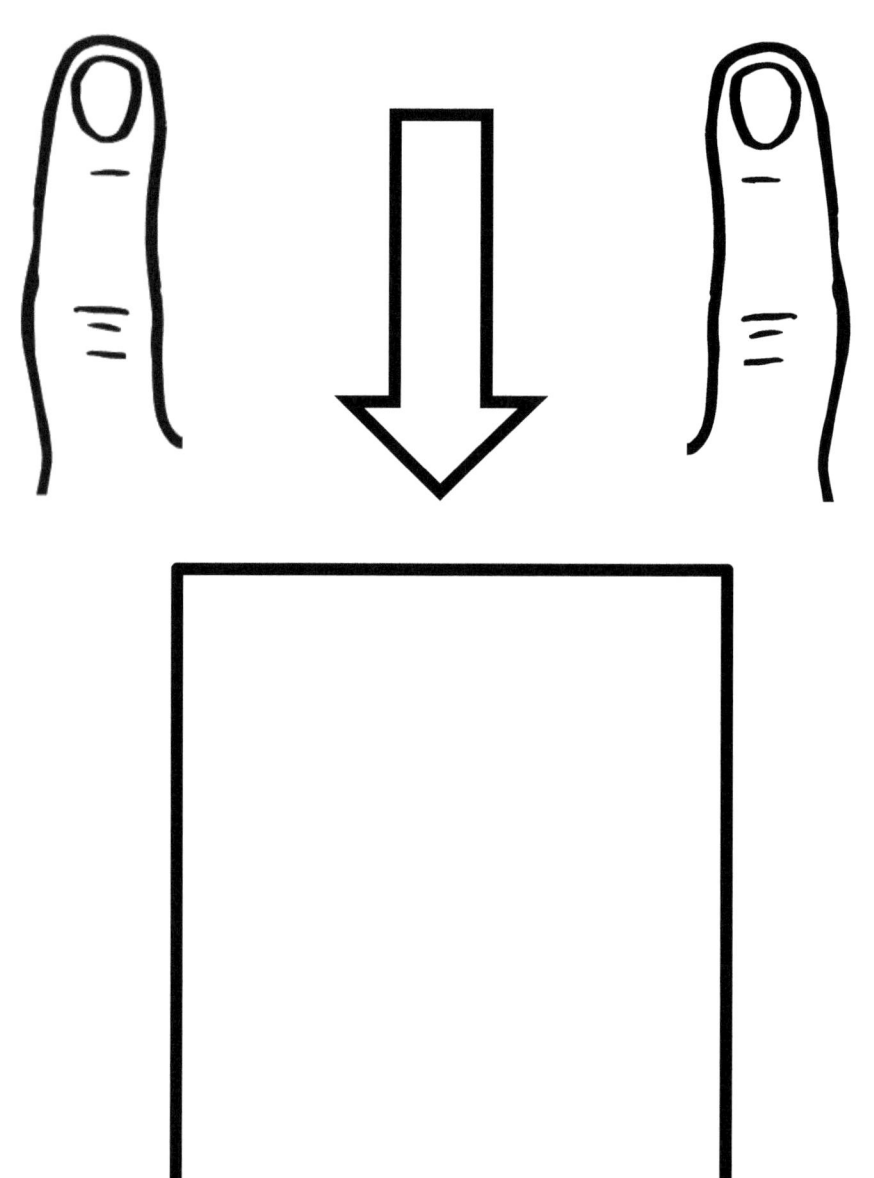

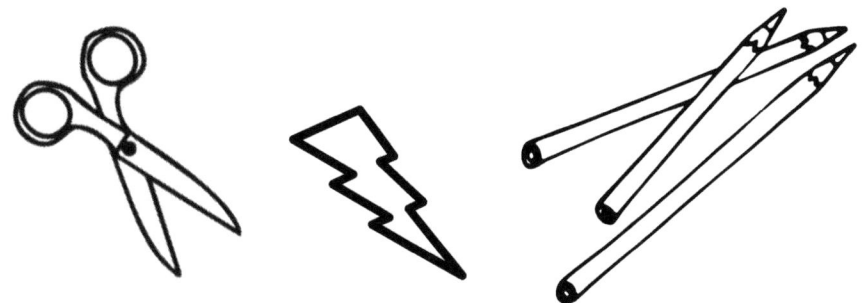

FUCK UP THIS PAGE!
PAINT ON IT WITH CRAYONS!
CRUSH IT!
FOLD IT!
TACKER IT!
PUNCH IT!
TEAR OFF PIECES!
SCRIBBLE ON THEM!
CUT THEM!
BUT LEAVE THEM IN THE BOOK!

What don't you like at all? Describe it exactly, leave nothing out and write everything down!

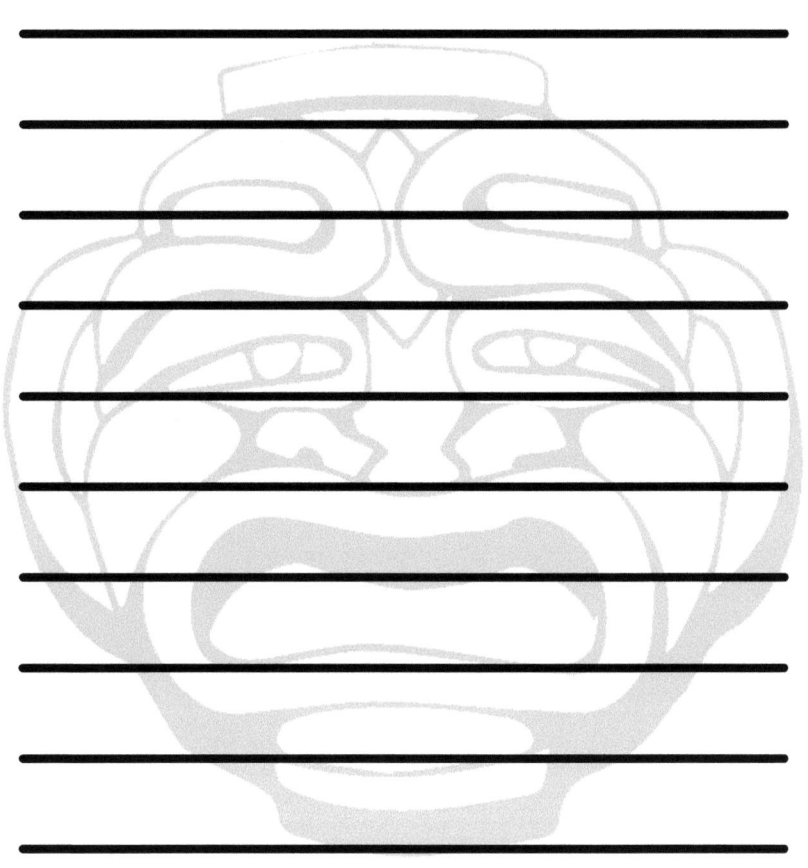

_____

_____

_____

_____

_____

_____

_____

_____

Stick all the price tags you can get your hands on, here!

Drown this front and back in perfume!

Take this book in both hands and slam it with great force on the table without letting go. Make a loud banging noise. Repeat this 30 times!

Put the book outside with these two pages when it rains and let it showing upwards rain! Or hold it under a jet of water for a short moment.

Clamp your pen between your middle finger and your index and ring finger and write the numbers 1 to 10 on this page!

Put paper clips on the three edges of this page. Then staple the paper clips in place.

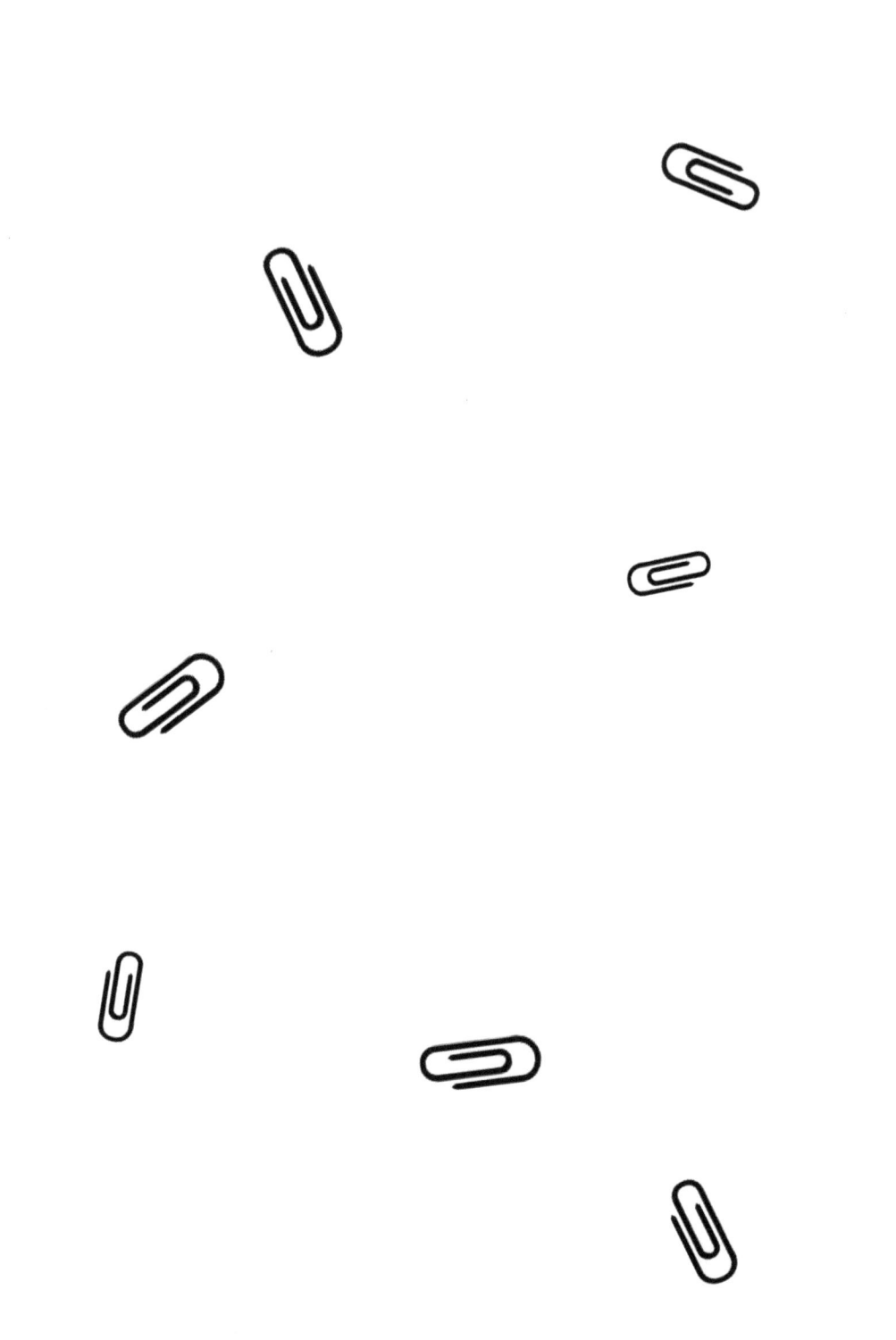

Glue an old DVD or CD onto this page!

GLUE STICK

Draw an unholy mess with a pencil. Create a drawing chaos. Make a good impression!
Then, erase everything, so that the page wrinkles and the pressure marks remain visible.

Memorise the position of the stars. Then take a pencil, don't look at the page and try to connect the stars with lines with each other!

Drop the book directly in front of someone you know and ask that person to pick it up for you!

Thank the person kindly for picking it up and look him/her in the eye for a long time.

Remove this page from the book and completely crumple it. Unfold the again and tear off both corners. Then glue it onto the smooth corners page and as best pages back as you can and stick it out back into the book!

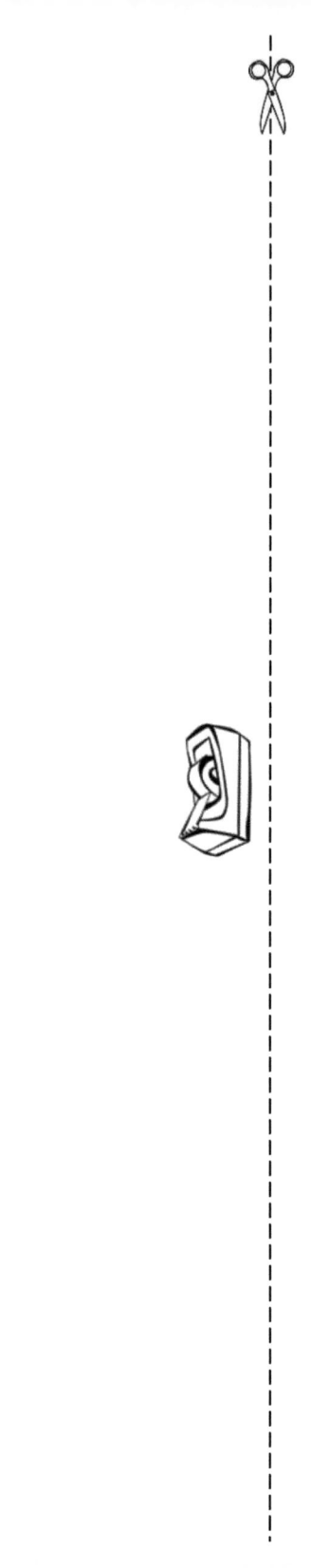

Blindly draw a stick figure on this page by holding one hand in front of your eyes while drawing.

Use this page as a money box. Stick as many coins as you like in the picture frame. Use transparent adhesive strips.

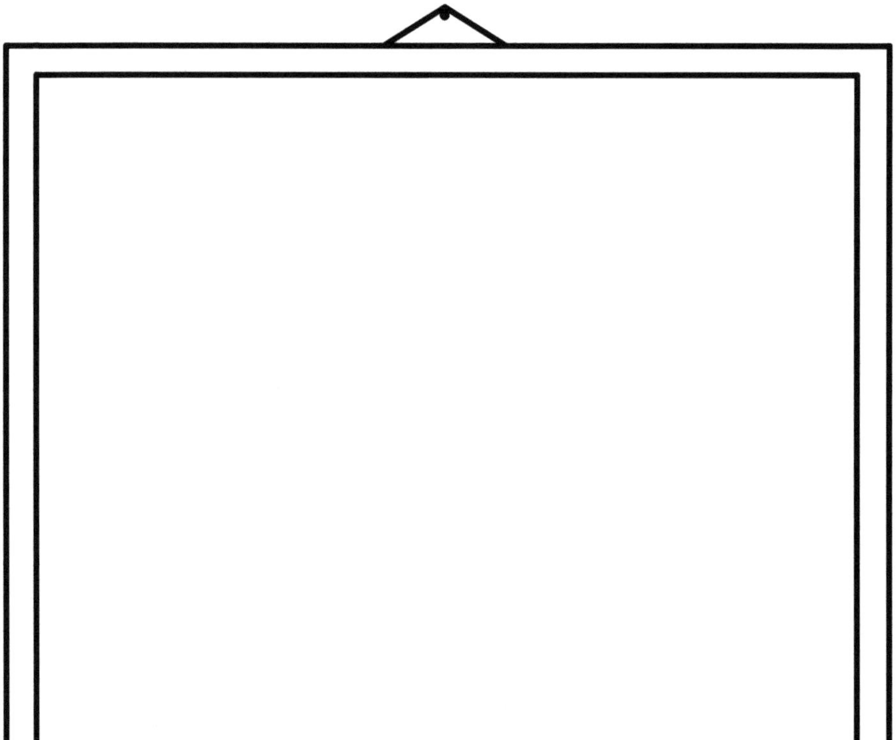

MAKE

A

TOMORROW!

FOR

PLAN

08:00 h _____

10:00 h _____

12:00 h _____

02:00 h _____

04:00 h _____

06:00 h _____

08:00 h _____

Drop the juice of
your favourite fruit
into the four
forms
on this page!
And write
the name
of the
fruit
underneath.

Dip a marble in ink over this side in ink. repeat this several times over. Let it roll times but repeat this several change the colours.

Draw random lines on this page with a ruler. Take a pair of scissors and then cut along these lines. Be careful not to cut anything off the page.

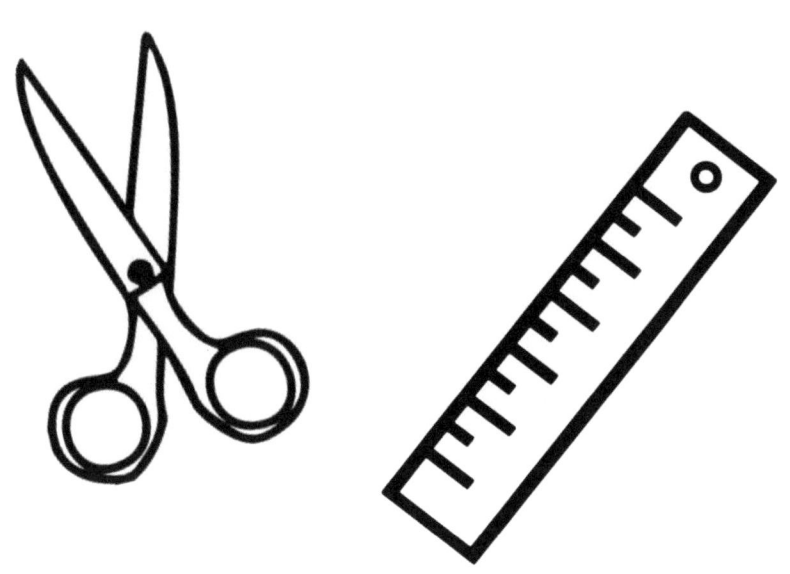

Take a stapler and staple the first letter of your first name to one edge of this page.

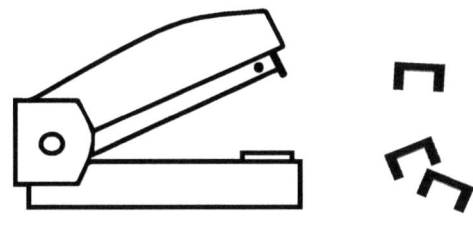

Example letter A

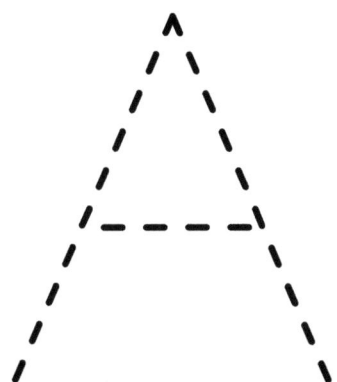

Pluck the fluff off your jumpers and glue it into the circles. Group the fluff by colour.

REMOVE THIS PAGE FROM THE BOOK AND USE IT AS A COASTER FOR YOUR DRINKING GLASSES. MAKE SURE THAT THE DRINKING GLASS IS INSIDE THE MARKINGS AS BEST AS POSSIBLE. IF THE PAGE HAS VARIOUS MARGINS AND STAINS, STICK IT BACK INTO THE BOOK.

Back

Take photos where you don't like the way you look and you can do without, then cut out individual parts of yourself. Put them together in a funny way and paste your work here.

Collect dust with your fingers and wipe it into the circle until it is completely covered.

- - - - - - - - - - - - - - - - - -

Create a book pocket!
Glue along the dotted
lines and press this and
the next page together!

- - - - - - - - - - - - - - - - - -

Cut out your favorite magazine advertisement and stick it on this page!

Remove this page from the book. Cut off the part marked 'bead'. Form a small ball out of this!

Then place the page with the back (playing field) facing upwards on a flat surface.

Place the ball in the starting position and then flick it towards the goal. If the ball stays in the goal, you win. You have ten tries! Then stick the page back into the book.

small ball

GOAL

START POSITION

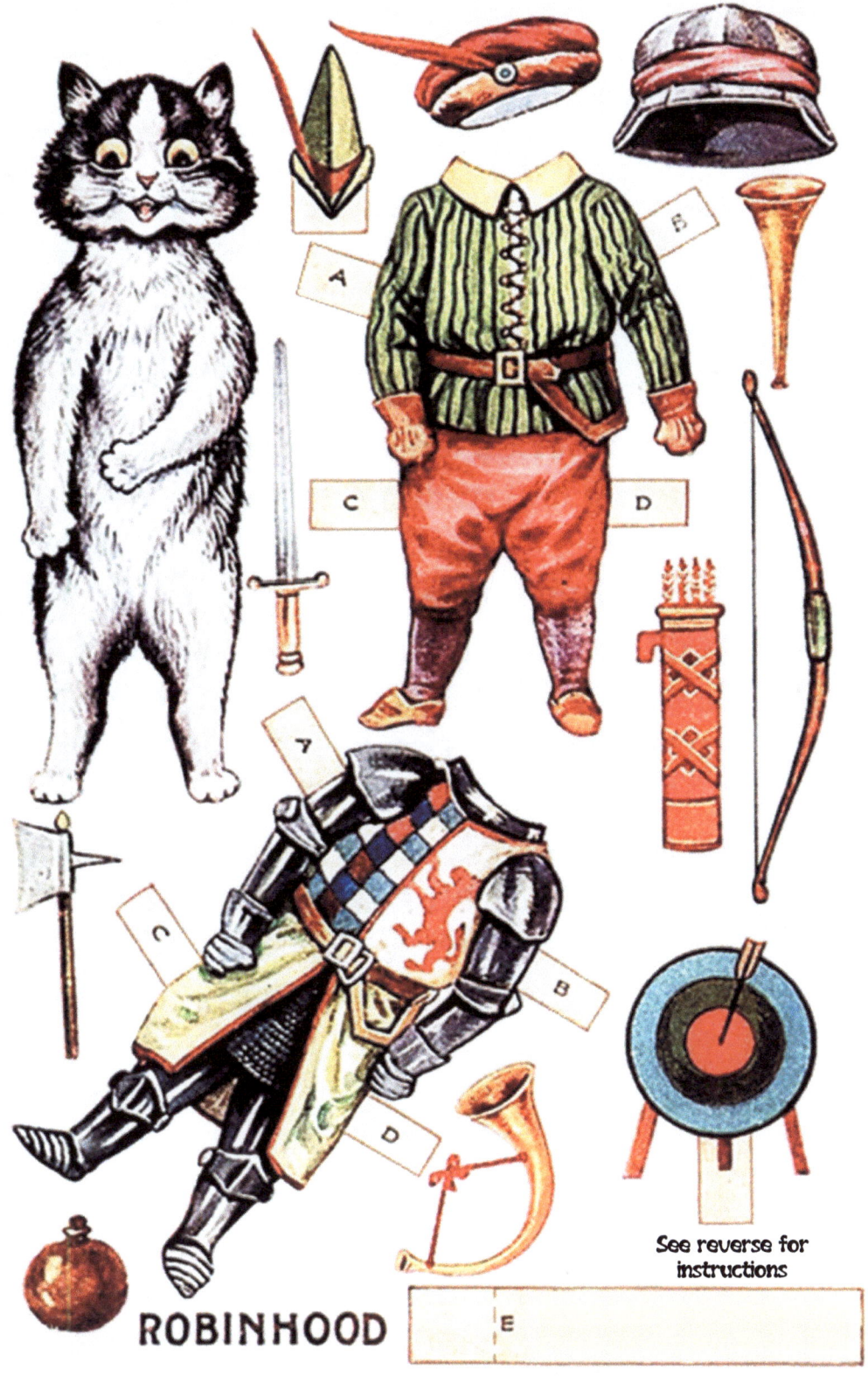

A

B

C

D

C

D

A

C

B

D

See reverse for instructions

ROBINHOOD

E

Robin Hood
Cat figure to stand on

INSTRUCTIONS

Carefully cut out the cat with scissors. Then the headgear and the small suits, making sure not to cut the small tabs A, B, C and D. To dress Robin, bend the small tabs A and B back around his shoulders and then C and D. To put on the headgear, cut an opening at the point marked with a thick black line. To make Robin stand upright, cut out the brace marked E. Then bend the dotted line forward and stick this brace to the back, directly between Robin's shoulders.

of your toes.

Place your bare foot on this side as best as you can. Trace the outline

Ask someone you know to draw something which characterizes you onto the page.

TAKE COOKED SPAGHETTI AND STICK IT IN THE WHITE FIELD OF THE HEART SO THAT IT FORMS A CLOSED LINE AROUND THE BLACK HEART.

MAKE TEN SMALL BLOBS WITH KETCHUP IN DIFFERENT PLACES ON THIS PAGE AND THEN CONNECT THEM BY SMEARING THEM WITH YOUR FINGERS!

Take a pencil in each of your left and right hands and draw a line through the two channels with both pencils at the same time, without drawing over the side lines.

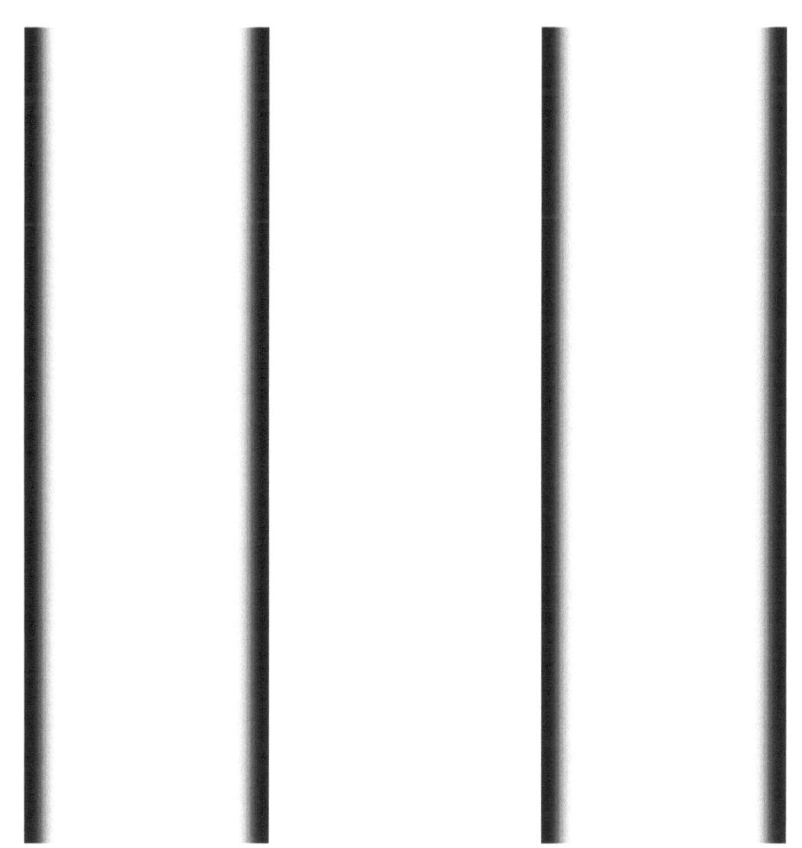

REMOVE THIS PAGE FROM THE BOOK! SAY GOODBYE TO IT POLITELY AND THEN BURY IT.

Mark all the white squares in the picture with a small cross. Count them as you do so!

What is the most boring thing that has ever happened to you? Draw a moon face to match the feeling you experienced.

Hold your pencil between your thumb and little finger and draw a stick figure!

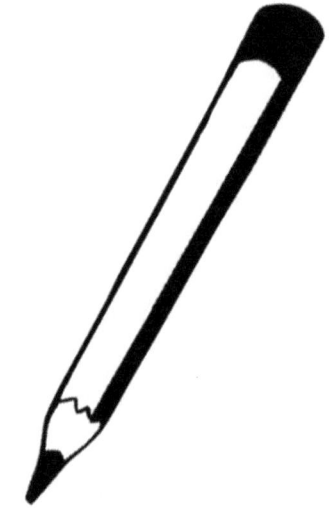

TAPE THE FRONT
AND BACK OF
THIS PAGE
COMPLETELY
SHUT!

**TAPE THE FRONT
AND BACK OF THIS
PAGE COMPLETELY
SHUT!**

TAPE THE FRONT
AND BACK OF THIS
PAGE COMPLETELY
SHUT!

Time for a creative break. Colour this colouring picture. Make sure that you do not paint over the lines. There should be no white space left at the end.

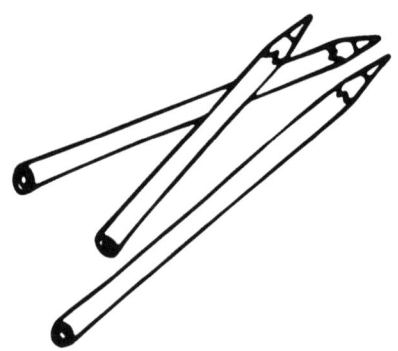

Put the book on your head. Now go to the toilet and come back without dropping it.

On the next page, draw an infinite line, always as close as possible to the edge of the page, without setting the pencil down. The line must not cross itself. The dot marks the start.

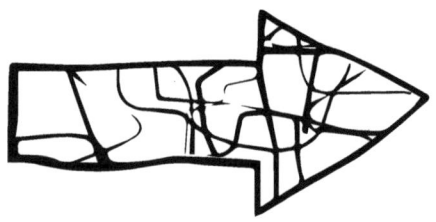

Write the first names of your three closest friends or family members backwards in the arrows!

Use the form on this page as a postcard. Cut it out, write a short joke on it, sign it and then drop it in a friend's letterbox! See what the reaction is!

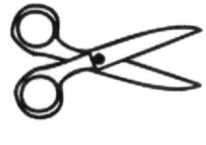

Call someone you like, press this book page in front of your mouth and explain what you are doing!

IMPRINT THE OUTLINE OF YOUR HAND IN THE AIR. MAKE SURE THAT ONLY THE TIP OF YOUR THUMB TOUCHES THE PAGE!

SLOWLY DROP SOME DROPS
OF WATER ONTO THE SHEET!
TRY TO HIT THE MARKS AS
YOU DO SO. THEN PAINT
AROUND THE DRIED EDGES
WITH COLOURED PENALS.

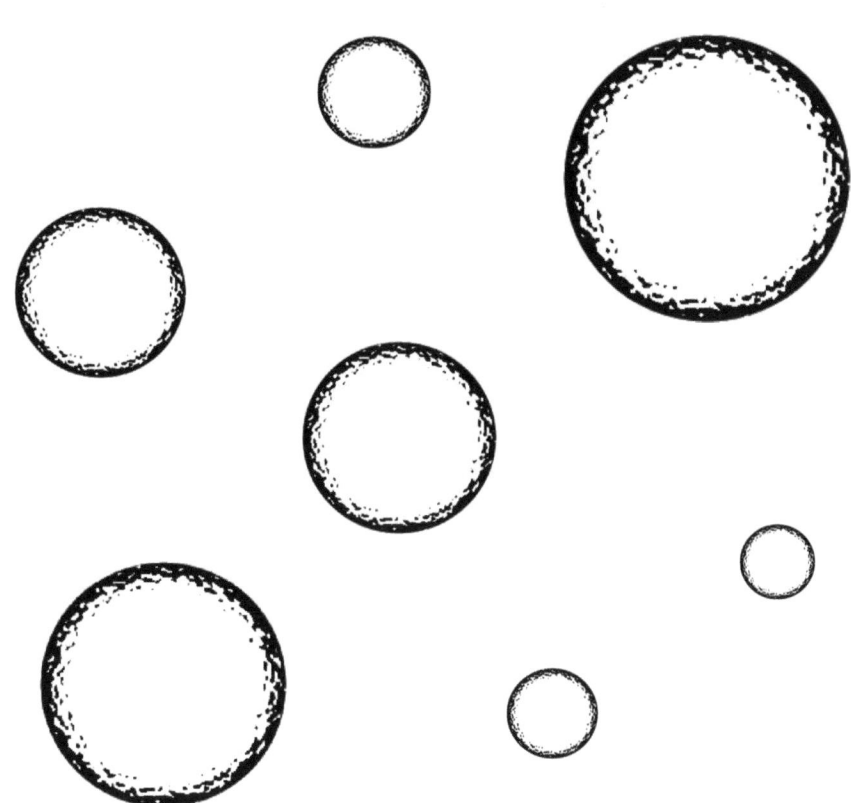

Remove this page from the book. Poke holes in the marks! Put a long, sharp pencil through the holes so that all the holes are pierced with this one pencil without tearing the page! Then glue the page back into the book.

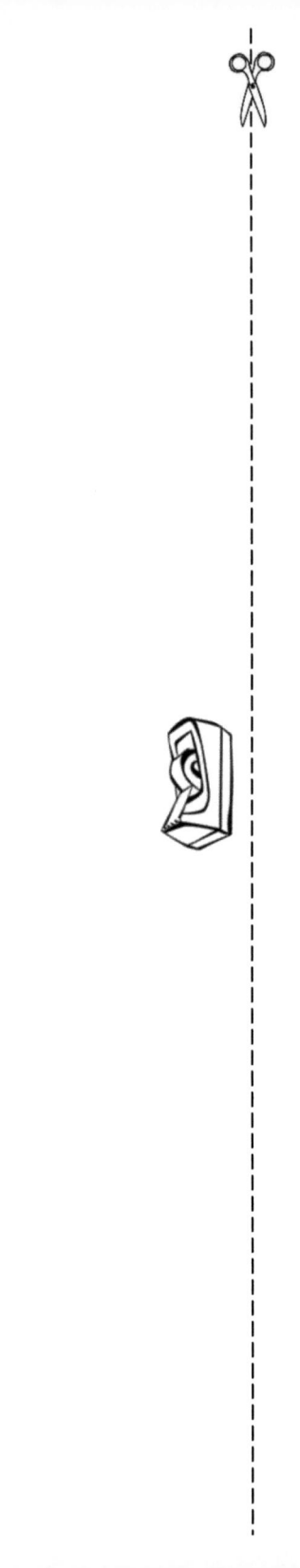

LAY THE BOOK OPEN ON THE FLOOR AND JUMP ON IT 25 TIMES WEARING SLIPPERS OR SOCKS. TURN THE PAGE AFTER EACH JUMP.

Take some newspaper and cut out words that you like best. Stick them on this page and do this until there is no blank space left!

PAINT A BEAUTIFUL FLOWER IN THE MIDDLE OF THE CIRCLE AND GIVE THE PICTURE TO SOMEONE YOU LIKE!

Stick a photo of yourself on the form and fill in all the details. Then cut out the card along the dotted lines.

MAKE

ID CARD!

YOUR

Titel:

_____

_____

Photo

Name, first name: _____

Street: _____

Postal code: _____

Town: _____

Ident number: _____

NMO

Cut the sheet along the dotted lines and mix the snippets. Then try to put the square back together!

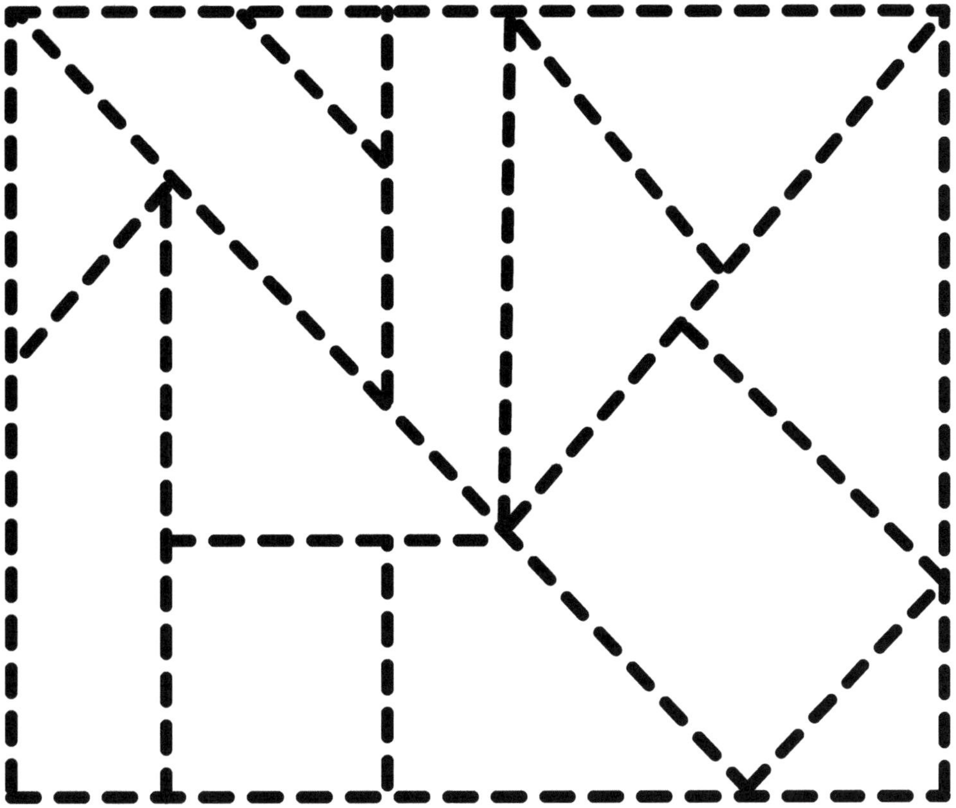

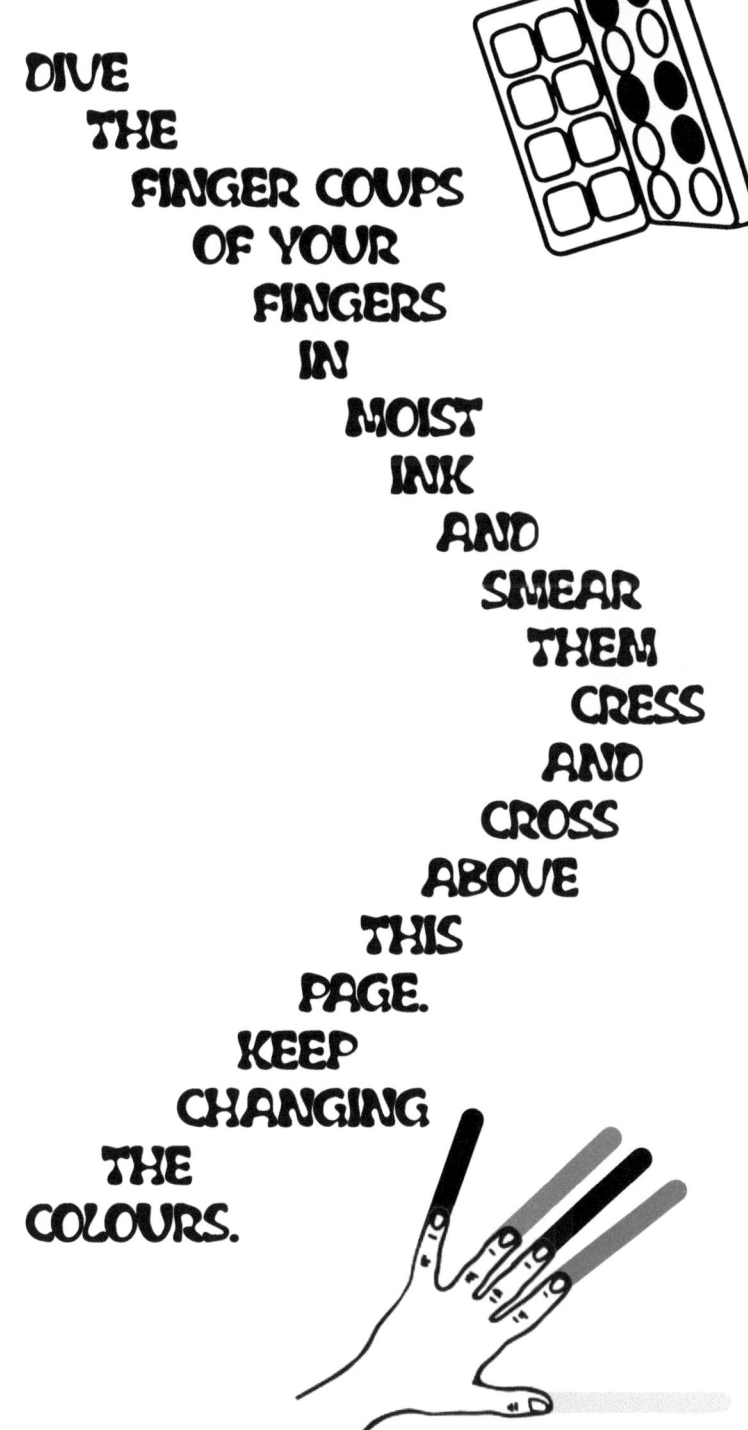

DIVE
THE
FINGER COUPS
OF YOUR
FINGERS
IN
MOIST
INK
AND
SMEAR
THEM
CRESS
AND
CROSS
ABOVE
THIS
PAGE.
KEEP
CHANGING
THE
COLOURS.

Cut out the triangle exactly along the dotted lines and try to estimate how many times it fits in the various shape. Write your estimate on each form. Check your estimate by trying out how many times it actually fits into each shape without overlapping.

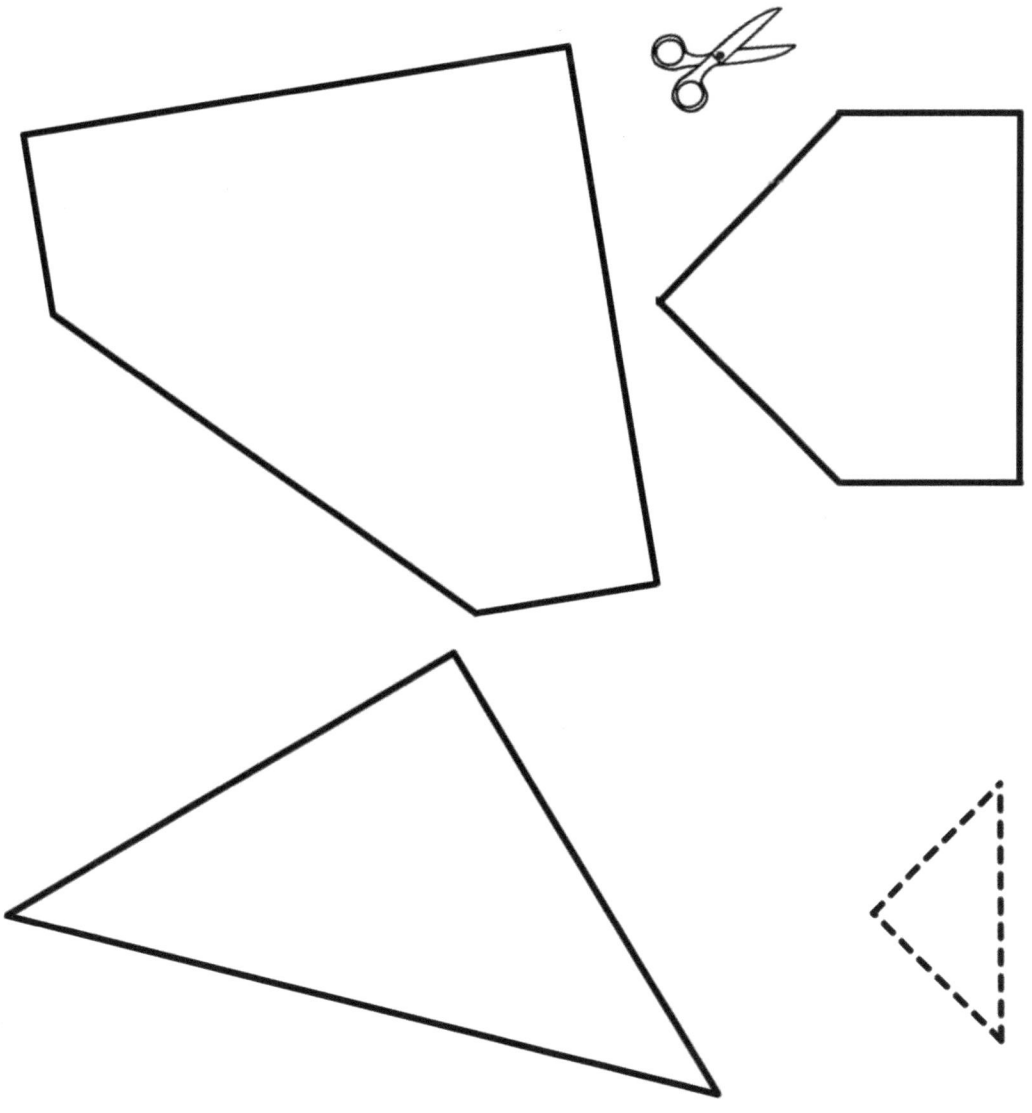

Make your own watermark! Take some margarine or butter and grind it between your fingertips.
Then use it to draw your watermark (e.g. a smiley face) in the box!

COLOUR THE FOLLOWING PICTURE!
GIVE THE FOLLOWING BODY PARTS
DIFFERENT COLOURS:
nose, eyes, wings, hands, arms, legs, feet,
tail, body, fangs, back.
ONLY USE COLOURS THAT CONTAIN
RED.

Save a leaf or a small flower for eternety and place it between these two pages in the book to dry and preserve!

Cut across the tip of a raw carrot. Use the carrot as a pen and write your name on this page with the juice that comes out!

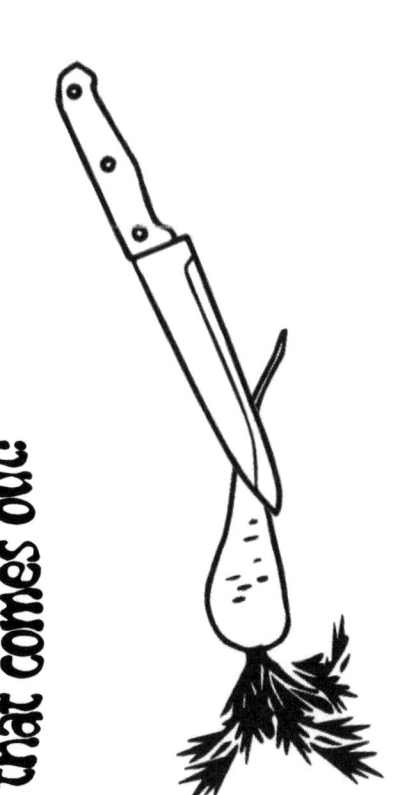

Write about you want to dream about in the thought cloud and put the book under your pillow before going to bed!

BUY THIS BOOK A MILLION TIMES AND USE IT TO BUILD THE EIFFEL TOWER ON A SCALE OF 1 TO 10!

Everything catches fire in this book. It's packed with sharply fried short and silly jokes, as well as well cooked cartoons on the subject of barbecuing that will set the gourmet heart of every barbecue master into ecstasy.

Start from the grill masters pole position into barbecue orgy of hearty humour.

Don't expect anything meaningful from this book. It is packed with lots of absurd and impossible riddles, twisted cartoons and jokes, and paradox scenarios that will shake the reader's worldview.

Buckle up for a mindbending rollercoaster ride through the mind.

Well done, gnome. This book is absolutely useless, but an entertaining occupation.

Thank you, master Roogle.

If you liked the book, I would appreciate a positive review.

End